"*tether* is a book of distances and intimacies, of letters never sent and dream talks and delayed communiques. It is a study of distance between us, between an astronaut and a poet, between lovers, between ourselves and each other, ourselves and ourselves. "We are the beached boat / with a hole in its hull," admits the poet. Each of us, even as "baby in a womb is a cloud." And yet there is so much love. And yet, everything that happens to us, happens for a purpose. And when one turns worthy, a giant squid washes ashore. It is this knowing, this insight into our distances (of years, of geography, of a space of a single day) here that I find compelling: "& how far / must you back away / from yourself / to see / yourself / as the Astronaut / secs/ Earth." Beautiful work."
— ILYA KAMINSKY

"Just over a full column of definitions for "tether" in the OED, among which are those that suggest diametrically opposite forms of fastening. It's fascinating to read through them, but not nearly so compelling as it is to read the poems in Lisa Fay Coutley's *tether*. We are tied, ensnared, and attached—in an especially intimate sense of that word—to everything that matters, which Coutley knows and makes us see and, in the richest sense of this word, *feel*. This is a superb book of poems."
— ROBERT WRIGLEY

"Is it desire, wonder, duty, or memory that keeps us most firmly tethered to the world, where "truth is every bird starving,"and we live in constant awareness of all the forces that threaten to break the bonds between us and our loved ones? A mother's death, a son's drug addiction, the disastrous world news filtered daily through the internet: how do we reconcile the painful events that define our existence with our hope for a more secure future? Through sinewy, sometimes hallucinogenic syntax that threatens to (but never does) spin out of control, *tether*'s poems examine a contemporary and very human paradox, in which we long to absent ourselves from our grief, while also needing to document our losses so as to ensure we won't forget. *tether* reminds us that we are formed as much from pain as from delight and that, in her ability to look back upon her past, upon today's terrible and compelling news, the contemporary poet is like an astr̲̅̅̅̅̅̅̅̅̅̅̅̅̅̅̅̅̅̅̅
"from a great height," a witness to wh
— PAISLEY

 Black
Lawrence
Press

www.blacklawrence.com

Executive Editor: Diane Goettel
Book and Cover Design: Zoe Norvell
Cover Art: "The Cloud Cage" by Jeff Faust

Copyright © Lisa Fay Coutley 2020
ISBN: 978-1-62557-812-9

All rights reserved. Except for brief quotations in critical articles or reviews, no part of this book may be reproduced in any manner without prior written permission from the publisher: editors@ blacklawrencepress.com

Published 2020 by Black Lawrence Press.
Printed in the United States.

tether

tether

poems

Lisa Fay Coutley

Black Lawrence Press
New York

For the loves of my life:

Cody, Channer, & Cooper

Contents

*

*

How

& how far

                    must you back away

    from yourself

to see

                    yourself

                    as the Astronaut

sees

Earth

    from the moon

                                    & how

far

                    is too far

*

It suddenly struck
me   that tiny pea   pretty
and blue   was the Earth

—Neil Armstrong

To the Astronaut: On Impact

I understand. I do. I used to lie back
flat against asphalt & take our moon

through binoculars—hands steady
as the dead's. I understand a planet is

its history of impact, what gets ripped
away & what gets left. The moon struck

from here flickers one brilliant sigh, one
small mouth stunned in the night, saying

nothing of two bodies about to collide.
Remember the way your legs dangled

over volcanic rock, the sun pressing
so heavy against the water we were

forced to bow? There's no prayer now.
Just histories that can only be told

given distance & time. Can't you see,
from where you are, how a target arches

to meet the body cast into its moment
of shared light? I understand the evidence

is the catastrophe. To be defined. You
chortled. You snored. You chewed this sky.

What Have You

Down here—forever projecting—
signs for signs for a sign for a woman

who kisses against the knife, but no one
sees her anymore. My son is the fist inside

the fist he's shaking at the rest of the world.
When he first heard his pocked heart homing

by rote, even its hollow couldn't show him
cage can also mean safe. Between us, clouds

are being torn apart by hands we can't see
or hold. Distance isn't the violent word we

mean if objects are always already absent.
What have you? What have you done

makes more sense. *What have you done for me
lately* doesn't make him laugh. What have I

done, he wants to know. Him. One of two
choices I made to hold change in the world.

II.

What have you *now*? I accuse the puppy

        & his boy responds—because desire

                Mom, because hunger—as if

he, too, could chew a couch cushion.

        I live here, with a head not made

                for hats, in blizzard country

where I accidentally slam the shovel

        against the asphalt & the dog

                barks & starts searching

for the other him & the other me. As if

        another us could be somewhere else

                where we sound better,

happier, full. My son says because desire,

        hunger, fifteen years already on Earth—

                this great gift he's certain we have

wasted & can never repair—words mean

        worse than nothing if we're thoughts

                unable to share pain

& wonder. What have you now to say,

        Mother, I ask myself, as I shove

                snow from an end to an edge

of dirt, bracing myself to throw, a language

so old—what *have* you?—taunting

me, the puppy arching, choking

on a chunk of anything, & I reach for a treat

from my pocket to dislodge it, thinking good

boy sounds so much like goodbye.

Winter: Tinea

or ringworm which I refuse to allow

      myself to Google Image   hell

it took me ten years to allow myself

      to consider how old you'd be now

mother shaking your denim bell

      in a kitchen always avocado

smoke whole notes our thrumming

      home lined by lilacs green apples

lake water behind forest before sounds

      so idyllic it's ridiculous

that I have both arms under a soggy

      box of records when the neighbor

squares her hands on my shoulders

      squeezes   remembers dad

(now dead) chasing you naked

      through the field waving

a pistol at your lovely   I must not
       have woken that night *Special*

Little Lady that I was for always taking him
       by the hand to the orange rocking chair

& spider swinging into that bright crushed
       not quite velvet where you weren't

well but weren't being beaten anymore
       so shhh quiet down now daddy

there's no reason to be so light
       house in the living room or living

loom as I'd say then   that's how
       little I was dad that's how little

you were   buttersoft hands
       around everyone's throat

eyes choked into
       every exploding color

less welts growing darker
       than dueling empty wells

so when she says *you're a miracle*

  Lisa Fay I think maybe but not

the same as a Nepalese baby found

  under rubble dust caked

over his eyes all messiah in the fire

  fighter's arms not like proof

of divinity but bones never broken

  though molded by aftershock.

ASTRONAUT: ON RILKE & JESUS

It's fair to say we've stretched

our *strengths between the two*

great opposing poles & God

is learning wonder & suffering

in the space between us. Why

should I be alarmed

to know *not one stone will be*

left, that all will be thrown

down, which is always

already straight from where I am

looking back or looking forward

toward our glass-dark home

with no answers. I've become one

pole & you an other, & in silence

emptiness. In loneliness

belonging. Coasting away is the way

to still the fragile gathering rivers

of light, gold you can see

nowhere but burning. Life collecting

like mold, where it grows most easily.

I fall more in love every day.

To Be Honest

I would rather say I have dementia
than depression, so I could still claim

center stage—blinded by an accent
light. If I bite the pink whistle yet

never blow, it's my fault. Right? I know
you know my grown sons know

they were not planned. Every event
that's saved my life has nearly killed me.

Honesta, in Latin, is a feminine noun
used rarely for Lady. When I drink

my iced mocha & type on my Mac
Book, I don't contemplate godliness

or the twelve-year-old girl whose gods
cannot stop the bleeding or the man lying

in prayer before & after he enters her
ruined temple (as his God wants), hoping

her stench will subside. I'm so afraid
that what has infected the world has

no smell & leaves no trace or it does
but all I can think to say is that I do

not want this dress anymore, though
I can't bear to let you wear it either.

THE DREAM TALKS

In its sleep we're the beached boat
   with the hole in its hull or you are

the wooden wheel in the dirt hole I am
   trying to fill or the leak just born

of the faucet is somehow holy & we are
   the forgotten prayer I keep yelling

stitch my stars again to the top of your hat
   then turn away just as rain begins

to clap through the trees echoed voice
   miles crying don't don't don't

make a fool of me to the birds you can't
   stand this steady drip   this man

with half a tongue playing the smooth flesh
   of his cheek so I am the cheek

so you are the gentle hand so we remember
   just as we are the dream sinking

the prayer him clucking his song his singing
   means nothing if nobody listens.

THE ASTRONAUT & THE POET

struggle to accept they are one

    another's to save or blame—

        the woman who left

her girl in darkness, or the girl a hand

    around a wrist, begging her woman

        through time. From a backyard

hammock she's not watching

    the robin's breast burning

        its trail of rust through sky

between them but dreaming it

    a lake, mid-tide, towing light

        between each of their shores.

She's given herself to twenty-two

    hours of sleep a day, letting go

        of gravity & holding her breath

underwater because she is the only one

    who has looked straight at her face

        without staying. She learned

early the fastest way to escape

    a plane sinking into a sea, has seen

        Earth unscroll its jigsaw topography,

could never forget their planet's curve

      & her, from such a height—dust

            at the bottom of a well, an island

slipping into itself, every granule

      of sand shoved from the top

            of the hourglass. Her winter

skin is snow-covered Scandinavia.

      Her rivulets are lakes are cloud

            are passing beneath a curtain

of fire she's falling through her hair

      doused her dress dancing her

            atmosphere resisting resisting.

Cloud Experiment

The way baby in womb is cloud cluster
      with an overbite   chalk outline

to the otherwise invisible water inside
      a night's sky   is not a storm

forming behind the white blinds
      where the cat readies herself

for every dark starling daring liftoff
      with her favorite poplar tree

which is little different than saying Dear
      Nimbus your underbelly's gray

as if it is true color is solid matter is not
      a shadow or density a reality

of ice so angered so close together
      that a mind can't rely on its eyes

so those of us still singing ourselves
      to sleep to spite the closet   need

the match dropped   the smoke trapped
      the miracle squeezed from its bottle

Truth is every bird starving   frozen berries
      at our hearts   pitchy roads   glazed

phone wires   mountains erect as dressing

    mirrors beneath sheets where a mine's

lights shine brighter than the moon's one

    scalpel scoop from darker weather.

TOTAL SOLAR ECLIPSE

Every shadow will sharpen
its blade against our strained
faces, plastic glasses & necks

craning toward the Mother
who refuses to be seen
otherwise. Mystery is her

bitch. Tight leash. Biting
tenor. Forgive me for how
wet I get just imagining

the day drained of itself,
the way city lights are fires
burning endlessly from space.

New perspective, same place.
They say Play-Doh in the palm
calms a child with autism.

A paperclip over a fingernail
for a nervous speaker. What, then,
for the woman each of us tries

to see, even in her hiding, woman
of untouchable temperature—all
that collapsed matter flattened

& fierce & always made to stay
at the center of every mistake
her children make—what could

soothe her? Does she remember?
Can she forget? Does she hope,
every time she cuts herself

to crescents, that we will see her
new, so alone with her own gravity,
giving all of herself to the dark?

Never & One Thousand Years Ago

Maybe even then, maybe especially then,

shamans knew the way, in the future, we'd be

able to look through glass into our own pores

& see stars, dust, the skin as terrain like any

other forcing forward through complete dark.

The way only years later, & now, you know

you never stood to leave that room, never rested

your plastic fork on its Styrofoam dish, still stuck

through the halved planet of a Brussels sprout,

never entered that blinding light & warm March

through doors parting before you without needing

touch. Never can you go back & hold your own

small hand holding hers heavy in a colorless bed

where every tethered star burns bright & dying

in her boundless mouth, open as a bird's, a mother

coaxing peas to her child. Never will you know

his name, the nurse reeling from her a clear, plastic

tube ribbed like sand, ribs of cloud, ribs catching
both corners of her mouth. Infinite. Wound

with tinder ahead. Wound with fire behind.

*

In a cage alone
a mouse almost always drinks
drugged water again.

The Letter I Never Send

Please stay with me until the end.
I know I should find another way
to begin, but last night I watched
Matt Damon play a lost astronaut
& thought of you. Who else could
withstand such solitude & grow
potatoes from his own shit? I kid
but listen—he was so loved, his crew
voted against their lives to bring him
home. At one point he was drifting
in utter darkness so close to the ship
just past his captain's reach, the Earth
or Mars like an endless mouth behind
him. Of course she got him. Of course
she was still tethered to the ship. I know
you hate it when I use stupid analogies
as if you don't know that bees are
now an endangered species & corn
causes cancer & babies are burning
in Syria & people are murdered
because our eyes want us to believe
color & *those* hearts fear *that* God &
there's no point going on. You know
more than I did when I was eighteen—
a single mother so far from the woman
who'd listen to a machine count down
her mom's last heartbeats & drive away
singing along to songs about lost love
that would never be about anyone else
again because love is love is love is love.
Listen, I don't know how else to say it—

before this woman was made to drag
that insatiable wound, she was tethered
to some small moon in her lap cut but not
cut from inside her. He was her gravity.
You are. Please look away from Mars
dangling so angry in so much darkness.
Look at my hand. Take the rope.

To Astronaut: On Fall

& now even leaves are surrendering
their last drops of water final burning

colors to the ground   & now I can see
the house across our lake yet I cannot

wait another staring moment for snow
to hold still the birch branches to cover

the truth of these vigilant trees   it's more
than I can take   our water is still blue

just deprived of light   along the shoreline
deer tracks in sand are hearts cleaved & marching

not away   I've built a blind from the dock
I pulled to pieces   cross-legged & armed warm

to watch moonrise bright rock at lake's bottom
one more blurred surface that I cannot walk.

Duplex

From the other side of the wall I hear
the woman who could just as easily be

me in my bathroom repeating *I am*
forty forty I am forty like a rehearsal

for the next man who will ask her age
the way a mother must remind herself

your son is a homeless drug addict your son is
your son is a homeless drug addict your son

until it becomes real & she can pretend
that this day can be different from the one

that came before or that will come after
her in those moments before sleep

when she hears thunder & pictures him
chin-up in a mummy bag in that city park

where last night she had his dinner
delivered to him & felt the earth spin

even further out of control & her life
she is sure is at least half over though

he doesn't even have a mummy bag just
a pair of sweats a t-shirt a ratty blanket &

she convinces herself this is his last meal.

ASTRONAUT AT THE WINDOW

Egg against. Flecked paint. Water locking
around a dime. Some wish. Some universe

in a different math. She lets her shawl fall
from her shoulders, devouring the bed.

Constellated freckles, relentless shores.
Even stars refuse to let go sometimes,

chloroforming every mouth, drowning
every eye. Lightning stitches its clouds

to its storms, pale bruises for drifting ships,
track marks for destinations. Earth the blue.

Earth the small. Earth the mapped—line
drive into the brilliant gauze, unraveling

bandage, rooting
                    pulse.

OF COURSE

I need to believe in love

    when my youngest son

        says he cannot fall

asleep without his *girl*

    because he's 18 & the word

        Xanax is a foreign planet

populated by Palindromes

    in eternal Ouroboros & my son

        can no longer sleep on Earth

Of course nothing I say will

    make sense not the weight

        of the heart he's dug dull

knifed from his chest & left

    on a filthy picnic table

        in the park where he lives

swinging days into oblivion chain

    links digging into the thinning

        meat of his fists not unlike when

he was too boy-eyed to see clouds

    show us so many ways to shape

        shift dying without dying

SENSORY DEPRIVATION FLOATS

Because the week I turn forty, a giant
squid washes ashore. It's the week I want

to say water cannot help anything, reaching
without touch, without hold. Pushing away.

This week, its twenty-third storm this year
plumes China & I never smell rain's metal

or know the impossible cold of the same
wet clothes against my heart & my legs

flood-deep for days. Dream of that cave
where stalagmites stand forever without

knowing the pink disc singes the slate
sky & the light divides & conquers

the greatest lake inside you because
forty   & still you cannot forget

love as another word for longing
to float, deprived of sense, robbed

of that manhole lid in your chest
pulsing midair & the weather in that

cave all your own, your own cloud
suspends while every drop of water

falling salutes. Who will miss this
me in that city of dripstone? Imagine,

kraken leaving such a hole by leaving
we celebrate life in *sound- & light-*

proof pods that host sensory deprivation
atop buoyant, body-warm saltwater this

week & last week & next because you
are the you who you wish to forget.

LEASH TRAINING

means trying to make the dog wear blinders
by shoveling fried hot dog bits in his mouth

that—jaws-open & yawn-wide—is now the size
of a dinner plate sailing toward a woman's face

as she rounds her car to enter the bank
or a small boy pedaling his bike to the beach

baby toddling with kite ANOTHER DOG
swinging children who'll probably strangle us

with pigtails or tall grasses or they harbor
every barking friend he can hear all night

all drops of chocolate in the baking cake
he'll never eat if it doesn't fall to the floor

& who can blame him his lunge & buck
at a leashed end for wanting to blaze

an aspen grove after a herd of elk when
I can't make myself ignore a single detail—

the way you said my name or toward the end

breathed *yeah yeah yeah* until you simply didn't

BLUE SKY THINKING

& who among us isn't magicked
> into being, & what isn't written
>> into the mind's folds

like mushrooms to the touch. The king
> of clouds is interested in nothing
>> but clouds, which is uphill

work & surging like a wave. Why
> should anyone agree that this
>> endless succession of cloud-

less days would be boring? We reach
> & reach & do nothing but burn.
>> Tell me to pay attention

to what's happening above, & I'll show you
> a woman cut in half by a window.
>> No matter. Fog is only light

scattered, the way a silencer makes
> room behind a bullet in a gun.
>> Food prepared from fish

is just *fish*. This mind, this blue day, sky
> full of galoshes & rain, this curtain
>> I never stop pulling. I envy

the tree its last curve of snow, the cloud

its slip of ice, simple

receding.

CATASTROPHIC THINKING

1) Have you tried guided mediation?

Descend the stairs slowly   one   by   one   nothing
but waitlisting   no love tumbling
blonde beehive over block heels down basement steps
no father shoving wife   mother
shoving son   son shoving mother   learning his growing
legs can take the stairs in threes
until the top where he can lock her in a chokehold.

2) Have you come up with a plan for how you'll manage your anxiety?

It takes eight minutes to search 25 words. Exhaling
purges more toxins than urinating. Running is not
as good as climaxing but can be better done alone.

3) What if you allow yourself 15 minutes/day to worry about X?

I was forty when I fell in love
with the Catalpa Tree—leaves
like hearts & fruit like daggers,
blossoms like spilled popcorn.

This does nothing to erase lilacs
& green apples from my scaffolding.
If your son is afraid to use the phone,
Facebook is skywriting. If he is paranoid,
snapping turtles are the best messengers.
If he dies—hear that whistle blowing?

4) Is that worry rational?

Rooted in reality? A mother breathing
bile on a bathroom floor? A son
sobbing on the other end of a county
jail line? A moon growing only so
whole before she whittles herself
again into unshakeable darkness.

INSTRUCTIONS

for Adam Gray

When you wake strange in your bed into that bald moment
       when the world's two kites aren't tethered to a hand

or tangled by visible line she's awake before you frying eggs
       in that old black pan swaying to her own low song

church bells on a Tuesday morning a roof pushed sideways
       against heavy rain that gray sky you aren't aware of

breathing   Before the past steps into focus   Before you notice
       every empty noose of this first morning without her

is a kitchen full of kites & wire   lie still
       sometimes we're all too tired for sight.

THE WRONG WISH

When breathing is the only thing
    between me & relief, grief is
        winning. I'm not so simple

I can't see that. I cannot change
    that the same crows came back
        screaming by the dozens

to my dying tree the past three days
    just as our sun was backing away
        from a half moon like a scalp

bandage worn through. You would like
    to know why I smile at its wound
        or this growing murder of crows

like they know me. How can I tell you
    I've never felt more seen, so alone
        only a body unimaginably far off

feels most close. Maybe that's what
    the untouchable have to teach us.
        I keep trying to remind myself

even the raven got it wrong. For all
    its prophecy, it couldn't know how
        dark the telling would go, that no

god would ever look at it the same.

        Truth is the enemy of any heart

                gripping the wrong wish. If

your son would sleep. If his wide eyes,

        his cracked lips. If he won't stop talking

                so you can't hang up. If you try to

memorize every inflection, just in case.

        Every word hurts. You can't hear

                enough. If you don't let him go

eventually he will see your love

        is killing you both. *You are dumb*

                as fuck, he will end things,

as if you didn't already know.

        Some say crows come in kindness

                in times of grief. Others see

only their darkest need. In one myth

        the raven paid with its silver to save

                us. Apollo stole it in anger

in another. If your son is just another

        wounded animal trying so hard

                not to cry for fear of being

found alone, crouched in darkness.

        Simple trail. Scent of blood.

                If Earth must force us

to learn early to bare our teeth

    when we feel most tender. If even

        stars aren't more than hunger.

*

The dog sleeps alone
curled in a tight fist loyal
to your dirty clothes.

DELAYED COMMUNIQUÉ TO ASTRONAUT

First thin skin of snow stop so white

    the breaking wave against its slate

        sky so close to its lonely

end again always stop sorry I haven't

    written in days stop I found myself

        telling the puppy he's lucky

& cursed to never feel compelled

    to hold his face against the wind

        just to watch the futility

of water rushing toward shore

    only to be thrown back & in

        stop to know that complication

is beauty I said & he showed me

    I'd never understand the simplicity

        of chasing a leaf though I've been

in love stop I thought I had nothing left

    to say stop there is a girl behind

        the birth of words inside me

stop she's waiting to forget her name.

BACK-TALK

So what. So you whittle away
at some endless road of homing bones,

rabbit queen of a coyote town, drifting
like influenza over the chainlink breath

of birds. So nothing will ever be
as it seems. The way baby in womb

is cloud cluster with an overbite,
chalk outline to the otherwise

invisible water inside a night's sky.
Lean with the precise if bent torso

of a Japanese Elm & hover above him,
gripping the thinning & sunworn thread

of love's plaid shirt. Water recedes. Weeds
will grow taller than any man you kiss here.

On Distance

Given two points, you can always plot them,
      you'd say, not knowing there are three
            days worth of clouds in one sky

& morning is a measurement I make
      by a thousand gray sails, warring
            toward a singular wind, hidden

horizon. Romantic, isn't it? The most
      common mistake—mismatched values,
            mishandled pairs. Distance is

farness is between two points is numbers
      describing how apart. Translation,
            rotation, rigid motion. Map for me

again across my back the shattered glass
      of affine space. Repeat there is no point
            of origin. I can't even walk the shore

anymore without calling all oblong rocks
      planets crashed but congruent at low tide.
            I'm not even sure what that means.

I know that the equation for warmth
      is one bent spoon diagonal to one queen
            bed. I know the story

is the problem & the solution if x & y

       orbit at different speeds around the same

             mailbox given an equal inner gravity

toward the other's voice, which is to say

       200,000 miles might be the length

             of our driveway if want, if not A,

waking every day next to B, praying please

       please do not touch me & staying that way.

SHELTER: MICHIGAN

Ben says it's like any other house
except twelve men share two rooms

in simple bunks not unlike barracks
& every morning he must trudge

the gauntlet of friendly, extended
booze bottles bagged & begging

him not to focus on the fall leaves
last-gasping en masse on the walk

to the gas station where he'll relieve
himself & scrub his teeth with balled

paper toweling until his gums bleed
or half the Happy Birthday song.

He wants me to circle *yes* or *no*
because his life has become unsafe

& what he needs most is an ankle
break woman who'll open the fridge

now & again so he can see the light
still exists inside them both. I won't

tell him yesterday I lost a patch
of hair on the top of my scalp

but refuse to name it until I know
if it's not alone. Cryptic Crop Circle.

Solar System in Bald. He wants me
to believe he met Jesus in Memphis

after his car went dead & he forgot
& forgot & forgot to feed his dog.

He has provided temporary refuge
from rain & rape, he says, but why

shouldn't we be each other's cover.
Why not disguise the facts, adopt

new identities, have each other's
backs. He promises to aim his gun

at anyone who tries to harm a hair
on my *pretty little head.* He can pet

name me. Baby Great Lakes. Tiny
Idea Cluster. Little Target Practice.

Ways to Leave the World

same as the way a woman populates

        loneliness with new cuisine   skin   a man

                who isn't hers   here   I walk too

fast   so I can say I've been trying

        to forget   the path doesn't exist

                past drowning   past crossing

wires in an open socket   somewhere

        else   halfway means six more

                sections of clementine

the moon   oranged with burning   the music

        pain's locked inside its rock   listen   sing

PORTRAIT AS FACTS OF ENERGY
BETWEEN US

Alone, a human heart thrums enough

to light a tiny lamp or power a handheld

radio. Together, two hearts could charge

a guitar amp. In love, we burn the color

of a small sun & people orbit us even

when we need to be alone. We tend

our better health when we're in love.

Each level of energy registers higher

octaves than the next until we reach

the I-Thou, the rainbow, the golden

egg, & we know perfection within our

imperfection. Divine will is a blueprint.

A white line perforates the center of our

bodies, rooting us to the same space

of earth. I pencil into a lake. He buries

his dreads in a foothill cave. Intersecting

streambed, vortex, radiant cloud, little

television set. I want to watch myself

lost. I'll let him play the stronger field,

slam me against his frequency—other

half of this red secret we cannot keep.

CHATTER (WITH STELLAR REMAINS)

My friend's lover, who's older than her
father, emails a photo he took in Spain

on vacation with his wife. Scene sliced
in threes to draw the eye from cat

to cage to woman. We joke about
the cat, outside the cage, thin enough

to maneuver the bars, the woman
far out a second-story window to see

the cat, seeing the cage. We joke about
obituaries, how my friend reads them

if her lover hasn't called in a day. I explain
binary black holes, how one star isn't

visible without the other. She knows
a man who dresses himself in shadows

draws light like hers. She's eager to knot
herself to *tidal force* & *naked singularity*.

He tells her he is the cage in the photo.
I agree, I say—*may be the smartest thing*

he's ever uttered. It may be
his most lovely gesture yet.

Maybe She Didn't Mean

to say   but the man next door

          was cutting down trees making space

for a moon to have its way with a light

          & a dark letting the man & the woman

                    emerge   him dipping her so

mercilessly upon his wrist across the white

          triangle to the neighbors' roof   her so

                    taken by the pull of branches

& the fist of hair he holds at her

          head her chin tilted just a bit

                    more than she might like

otherwise   this suits her fine   this man

          this woman   birds thrown against

                    a sky of houses already built

ASTRONAUT SEES UPHEAVAL DOME

Little Love, from here you're a question
mark now. Star wound. Misnamed shape

through space where moons are christened
with myth & basins with men. Little Crater

of Mistaken Origin, Lonesome Ring in the Island
in the Sky made straight by stream-cut canyons,

your shocked quartz rises like bone broken
& holding tight the lightning behind the skin.

You were never the violence inside the tender
center of rock. Target, terminus, welt I know

my mouth could never predict, nothing led us
here but collisions I trace through such dark

floating hours. I hope you can know impact
as a random route through space & time,

that nothing can stop the rock dropping
to its water. Even the fist that rips earth

from earth cannot stay & cannot go without
pressing close against something just once.

50 Degrees

on the back of a motorcycle means fuck

this stare at the sun until the sky's an x-ray

where cumulus stills & a moon's sutured

to a lake like light from both ends of a needle

piercing the same fabric living twice

& dying once so easily wounded so quick

to wound   every letter I'll never send is

addressed to you there reflected & still

just one bright point parted love being

the word the poem doesn't want to say

broken on the back of a motorbike

arms around someone for warmth only

feels like the desire to live   doesn't it

won't you let it do you know how cold

DEAR JOHN—

you must know—is not a simple phrase
written on one of two bombs I can't stop

dropping inside me. That's all she wrote
is another way to say I would rather live

with my burning than sleep with my dead.
Keep putting your hand against my chest,

even if I refuse to speak words, you plead,
convinced I could lead any man to dance.

I need to tell you the truth—I'd rather
breathe my burning than love my dead—

but I'm trying hard to pretend I don't dream
of pirouetting into enemy fire. I might lie

in this bed forever bingeing *The Leftovers*
& never realize I'm not like the shut-in

who dies alone with no one to check her
animals that will certainly eat her. I am

her. I am the daughter who once taught
a neighbor girl how to shove someone

to the ground by repeating the move
on her over & again, though I never

showed her how to keep her footing.
This—Dear John—is to say the reason

you shouldn't love me now is the reason
you would've overlooked me then, when

you were already wise enough to know
the world held its knife to your throat

& it was everything worth kissing against.

*

hearts cleaved & marching
not away   even trees
fall in each other's arms

WIND TURBINE ERECTION:
A TIME LAPSE VIDEO

I'm watching in accelerated motion as men dig
a deep dish & fill it with the concrete needed

to hold the turbine's base, to steady the blades
it takes one train & six semis to deliver to these

Great Plains. Things could be as simple as naming
someone the small town police chief of our hearts

yet we love with the forgiveness of science.
Anyone who's not afraid has never crawled

to a rooftop to escape growing, poisoned water.
Don't say hope to me. Even a tree knows better

than to bet against windthrow. *Died unexpectedly*
always means it was their life to take & choice

is hope. Do you know how small a man looks
inside a wind turbine's shaft, gripping his tool

to bolt every, erect section closed? Of course
I worry for his safety. For the earth. The birds.

No one knows how many will die or when

my dog will go, but I can tell he'll go alone.

We're always about to bleed, my friend

& I agree—our bodies patterns of pain

for unsung songs. That's one way to see it.

See what can be seen, you tell me, as if

I'd been trying to take our picture from two

million miles away. I hope Earth destroys us

before we destroy each other, I want to say,

but how can I make you see a woman's right

to burn her temple with all her children inside.

LAKE PREDICTION

We know California will take it the hardest: losing

       palm trees is never easy. No one will speak

of the redwoods. As a community, we'll fold

       & unfold our sweaters, pack night

bags with the last of our peaches. We'll wait.

       We'll breathe but think of it only

when smoking. Eventually, the telephone poles

       won't hold, & we'll call a desert a desert

again. No one will bless the faucets or pray

       for hailstones to halve like human eyes,

so the baptism by thistle will go unnoticed. It will be

       easier that way—to say no one was watching.

Nalgene bottles will go fast & flasks even faster.

       By night, some will rediscover their hunger

for another hunt, so others will become prey, evading

       brandings, shackles, open roads. We'll trellis

mountains in groups, using fish bones for cairns, & when

dirt storms over us a second time, we'll hope

for locusts. A woman will claim she's seen trumpet vine

covered with golden husks in North Dakota.

We'll wait. No one will bless her pocket. No one

will pray for a stranger's empty shell.

DEAR MOM—

It's been an hour since the storm sirens
began, yet I've felt freezing rain for days.

Outside my window, the plastic bag
snagged in the neighbor's tree is filling

with wind then letting it go over & again.
I cannot stop breathing. It's been so long

since we've spoken I've given up trying
to remember the last words you slurred.

Your voice a broken shell I cut my ear
against. You & I both know I hope for

no ocean. Now that you're dead, do you
think love is wasted on the living? I have

pretended to look for you in every face
since I left the last room we breathed in

together. Remember when you dropped
your favorite dress at your ankles & stepped

into the street without me? Each night
some woman stumbled home & tried

to cook your recipes. Her hands just cut
you. I was seven. I promised then I'd never

let her hold me. My life began inside you. What
else is there to say? When I listened to a machine

beep your last heartbeat, I never rested my head
against her chest. Dear Mom—I'm still waiting

for that horse in my heart to stamp its hooves
again. I can drop a potted plant from my roof

a hundred times, though it takes just once
for it to learn to brace against the next impact.

I'm sorry the world made it so hard for you
to know the difference between a caress

& a closing fist. I'm sorry you left yourself
alone. Lonely. Briefly, today's rain gathered

on the slats of the deck, & I admired the sky
twice. Still I wish I didn't need to see the trees

dark as charred bones, poisoned veins. I'm sorry
I made you a disease I wasn't willing to admit

I had for so many years. I close my eyes & try
to summon your face—a hole blown through

the center of every floor in this endless sky-
scraper inside me. Sometimes, in the mirror,

I stick out my tongue & widen my eyes & cry
like a baby who needs her mother to see her

need, to be her initial witness, to prove she
exists, so she can stop hauling her body

from city to city, bed to bed, searching
for herself in the faces of strangers. When

the temperature finally dropped, the rain
froze a mosaic, angry fragmented second

sky the snow is working hard to cover now.
The sun never showed today. Still I feel her

setting. As a girl, I'd sit by the shore & study
her early bruise & her evening blood spilling

under a door to another room of the universe,

as if I knew every gray day to come without her.

The Letter I Never Send

always begins in error—dead for dear,
fear for terror, panic for dread. I mis-

use his moons to speak our violent birth
because to fill with fear is not to be

afraid. To anticipate danger is
not a sudden & uncontrolled punch-

to-the-throat response. It's just in my blood
to footwork circles around the way two

rocks cut like pocked hearts, embracing one red
force, can orbit at such different speeds,

always turning away. The night you left
so close to moonrise, I anchored myself

to that last sky, staring into the sun
until the day had become an x-ray

where cumulus stilled & our moon sutured
itself to our lake like light from both ends

of a needle, piercing the same fabric,
living twice & dying once. Reflection,

though, is still just one bright point parted. Love—
so easily wounded. So quick to wound.

To cherish, to treasure, staring with deep
affection is not departed, over

& out, absolute. I'll always tether
my desire to stay broken to you.

ASTRONAUT: ON FORGET

I can no longer think of just one
          true chair, one pure bed. The heart
               changes shape in space. I am

no longer mass defined by attraction.
          I sleep better here than I ever did
               there. You see me

battened to the ceiling & think up
          side down, but now is the ease
               of breathing underwater

where bones still fall but all belong
          to the sky. The only debris field
               here I weigh in candlelight—

one shadow for each season of can't.
          I've fastened your face to my wall
               of maps, so when I wake

from a place where the stillness of trees
          terrifies me most, I'll remember home
               also means to be ushered back.

Partial Eclipse, Hail

Molten horseshoe hung upside down
        against nothing but dark & then
                more dark. Space, you'll say—

distance, time. This evening, beneath
        some blooming tulip tree, not even
                the moon & sun make certain

a path to one smelted ring in the sky.
        Here, I know, holds a similar kind
                of darkness as there, all the blood

drained from the day, the sun cutting her
        self to crescents against flowers & leaves
                on this poplar, this concrete. Ache

is why I came here, to a roof's edge, witness
        to some celestial event, rare as looking
                without fear or shield, willing

to singe the small net of blood I've been given.
        Somehow, hail falls all around you, halving
                its white from its white. Believe me

when I say breathing is more than exhalation,
        that we'll always take in more than we can
                ever give back, yet somehow we keep

growing closer together, in lesser conditions,

spinning uncertain & dumb & out of time

until bone is skin is air is fire.

PINK MOON   SPROUTING GRASS MOON EGG MOON

fat searchlight moon   making small

    these mountains & every other

        face in a crowd   where I wait

to see those features I know

    by mouth   come into focus

        moon or locus   heart or waves

cresting across a hospital monitor

    screen   resisting the final say

        all late day   waiting   to know

you lonely bowling through cloud

    shocked pupil moon   tossed over

        red rock's shoulder

slammed up against night's pitch

    dark is simple   you moon   & even

        light sometimes   can only bury

its face in a back   between the blades

    of the one   walking ahead   walking

        away   & we all   tethered moon

LOVE IN THE LANGUAGE OF AVIATION

In which there exists no X or Y & Z
is for zoning & zeroing-in on the general
calculation of failure used to map our safety,

but let's face it: little is more fragile than this
act of juggling glass & metal along a false
horizon. Takeoff is something we must do

blind. What can hearts know of houses or road
signs needed for dead reckoning when traveling
at speeds the dirty side can never handle. Tension

means to grip firmly the control column. Caging
prevents the susceptibility of damage. Caution.
Warning. Emergency. Distress is the same

in every brittle language. Love is the coffin
corner: the heart, reaching maximum altitude
& top speed:: the moon, raising its blade

in a part of the sky you hadn't expected. Without
ballast, without static wicks, without calculating
true air speed, we barrel-roll forward, all hands

& knees, bracing. Up here, furthest upstream
of a moving object, what we cannot see of bow
& stern, we hear. Let it be less a snap or crack

than a boom when the waves mangle themselves
faster than normal toward us. We know the shock,
abrupt, its energy dissipating quickly. Takeoffs

equal landings, we hope, though we can never be
sure the earth wants us back. May we embrace no
failsafe, no reverting to home, no direct course.

Let our landings come through thunder & snow.
Let this rabbit roll us rough down a river of stone.

Informing

& a helicopter flat

           against the moon   constantly

hauling bodies. My foot

           is the shape of my mother's.

The lavender's at the door.

           Blind me. Take away

           my right. Tell me the smell of purple
you've never smelled before.

Astronaut, occluding. Forget what

           you can   forget

what you cannot. Take the curve

           of the earth at the roof

           of my mouth.

ACKNOWLEDGEMENTS

Many thanks to the editors of the following publications where these poems first appeared, sometimes in different versions or by other titles:

32 Poems: "Total Solar Eclipse"

Adroit Journal: "To the Astronaut: On Fall"

AGNI: "Shelter: Michigan"

The Alembic: "Chatter (with Stellar Remains)"

Anti-: "Pink Moon   Sprouting Grass Moon   Egg Moon"

Blackbird: "Leash Training"

Bennington Review: "Of Course" & "How"

Connotation Press: "Portrait as Facts of Energy Between Us"

Crab Orchard Review: "Astronaut at the Window" & "Back-Talk"

Crazyhorse: "Cloud Experiment"

Dialogist: "Love in the Language of Aviation," "What Have You," & "Blue Sky Thinking"

Ecotone: "The Astronaut & The Poet" & "Partial Eclipse, Hail"

Glass: "Astronaut: On Forget"

Gulf Coast: "50 Degrees"

Inter\rupture: "Informing"

Kenyon Review Online: "Delayed Communiqué to Astronaut"

The Los Angeles Review: "Wind Turbine Erection: A Time Lapse Video"

Narrative: "Dear John—," "Duplex," & "The Letter I Never Send"

Pleiades: "Dear Mom—"

storySouth: "To Be Honest"

Sugar House Review: "The Dream Talks," "Astronaut Sees Upheaval Dome,"&"To the Astronaut: On Impact"

Tupelo Quarterly: "Sensory Deprivation Floats" & "The Letter I Never Send" *Vinyl Poetry & Prose: "Winter: Tinea"*

"Of Course" was reprinted on *Verse Daily.*

"To the Astronaut: On Impact" was reprinted on *Verse Daily* and in *Cicada Magazine.*

Never & One Thousand Years Ago" appeared in *Thirty Days: Best of Tupelo Press' 30/30,* edited by Marie Gauthier, published by Tupelo Press.

"Pink Moon Sprouting Grass Moon Egg Moon" and "The Dream Talks" were nominated for Pushcart Prizes.

I am eternally grateful for the support and guidance I've received from professors, students, and staff at the University of Utah, with special thanks to Kate Coles, who worked closely with me on this book as it took root during my PhD program. To those professors and classmates who were integral in workshop and in my dissertation defense, where these poems first appeared as a collection—Kimberly Johnson, Jackie Osherow, Scott Black, Howard Horwitz, Erin O'Connell, Lillian-Yvonne Bertram, and Meg Day, among others—I appreciate your feedback and dedication.

Thank you to the National Endowment for the Arts Literature Fellowships program for awarding me a fellowship in 2013, which allowed me the gift of time I needed to refine this collection, to Marie Gauthier and Kirsten Miles at Tupelo Press for giving me the space and encouragement to compose many of these poems during two separate 30/30s, and to everyone at the Sewanee Writer's Conference for the gifts of time, distance, and encouragement.

Sincere thanks to the careful readers of this work: Chloe Honum, Tony Frame, Laura Eve Engel, Eric Smith, Traci Brimhall, and Sandra Beasley. And to those poets who have spent time with these poems and offered support: Diane Seuss, Ilya Kaminsky, Major Jackson, Robert Wrigley, and Paisley Rekdal. Diane Goettel, Kit Frick, Angela

Leroux-Lindsey, and everyone at Black Lawrence Press, I can't thank you enough for loving this book, for taking good care of her, and for ushering her into the world with such enthusiasm.

Strange though it may seem, I am most indebted to the Apollo astronauts who, in their brave efforts to explore new terrain, showed me how important it is to create the distance needed to see yourself and your place in things with a new perspective, to recognize the difference between the journey you thought you were undertaking and the gift that can come as a result of continuing to move toward curiosity and discovery, and to remember that looking back can also be a gesture of hope.

RANDY MATTLEY

Lisa Fay Coutley's first full-length poetry collection, *Errata* (Southern Illinois University Press, 2015), won the Crab Orchard Series in Poetry Open Competition Award, and her chapbook, *In the Carnival of Breathing* (Black Lawrence Press, 2011), won the Black River Chapbook Competition. Her poems have been awarded fellowships from the National Endowment for the Arts and the Sewanee Writers' Conference, a Rona Jaffe scholarship to the Bread Loaf Writers' Conference, and an Academy of American Poets Levis Prize, chosen by Dana Levin. Her recent poetry and prose has appeared in *AGNI*, *Black Warrior Review*, *Brevity*, *Missouri Review*, *Narrative*, and *Pleiades*, among others. She is an Assistant Professor of Poetry & Creative Nonfiction in the Writer's Workshop at the University of Nebraska at Omaha.